Never Wear Flip Flops in the Rain

Roisin Rzeznik

Copyright © 2012 Roisin Rzeznik
Copyright © 2004 Roisin Rzeznik

All rights reserved.

ISBN-13: 978-0615617435
ISBN-10: 0615617433

Dedicated to:
My Savior; My Light, My Refuge, My Rock, My Strength, My Rainbow, My Friend, My Hero, My Lord, MY EVERYTHING!!!!!!!!!!!!

-Roisin

CONTENTS

Acknowledgments	i
The Woman Cried	1
The Gift	2
Claddagh	3
I See You	4
Faith	5
Love of a Lifetime	6
It Could Be	7
Ultimate	8
The Greatest of All	9
Your Song	10
Love Without End	11
Destiny Bound	12
Forevermore	14
More Than	15
Beloved	16
Love From Above	17
Beautiful You	18
Shattered	19
Your Eyes II	21
Every Single Day	22
Very Special You	23
Genuine Love	24
Victory and Glory	25
I Love You God	26
The Dance	27
Faded Glory	28

Reprinted for Joe Elliott; in loving memory of Joe Sr.

© 2004 Samuelson; I Love You God
© The Bobby Sands Trust; The Woman Cried

All Rights Reserved

Used by permission

ACKNOWLEDGMENTS

Thank you to all of my beautiful children for their love and heartfelt contributions to my world and Jesus a Mere Image…

My sweet grandbaby

Bobby Sands Trust

Joe

My Grandmothers, Grandfathers, and Uncle Paul for their love, patience, and kindness

"Anam Chara, Domani è oggi…Amore Eterno"

My Extended family, whom love at all times…

You know who you are!

"Thank You"
Jesus

The Tolerant Twilight Singers

Roibeárd Gearóid Ó Seachnasaigh

Bobby Sands

"The Woman Cried"

Never Wear Flip Flops in the Rain

THE WOMAN CRIED
BY
BOBBY SANDS

From humble home in dead of night,
A flitting shadow fled,
The yellow moon caught sharpened pike,
Where the night shades danced and played.

A bramble clawed at trembling hand,
And a night owl watched unseen,
Through bog and glen a United man,
Marched out to win a dream.

Cold black water lashed and splashed,
And played round a tattered reed,
By dying embers, to God a woman prayed,
That the Gael might but succeed.

The silver nails of a rugged boot,
Scarred a lonely lifeless stone,
'Cross rambling hill he marched afoot
To fight along with Tone.

Six days he fought,
Midst dying piles of gory mutilated heroes,
And the English cannon roared.
Upon the ghosts of Celtic bones,
A nation's blood was poured.

Thousands fell in screaming bloody terror,
Whilst the informer hid cowering close by,
But there were none left amongst that bloody fray,
To hear the woman cry.

The Gift

This is a special gift
A gift from me to you.
If you are ever lonely or
Just feeling blue…
Hold this gift close to your heart.
Please leave it wrapped and tied
And know I think of you.
It contains precious love inside.

CLADDAGH

Do you still love
Have you ever wished
Is there a love
A love you miss

Another prayer whispered
A heart so empty
A soul full of unrest
Years since I've been caressed

I close my eyes
I see your face
Why have you left me alone
Alone in this place

I hear your voice
In every song-every note
To give it all for you
My choice…my choice

The pain never fades
God, can't you hear me!
The Pain still remains
God, set us free!

I SEE YOU

When our eyes meet
I see beauty
I feel complete

I look into your eyes
I see the greens of Erie
The sands of the sea
Flecks of burning embers
Entwined in a passionate dance
Randomly submitting
Each of their own accord

The beating of your heart
How could I ask for more

To never see your eyes again
Leaving my heart empty
Feeling like a plain ol' Jane
Never to know gifts of plenty

To be seen but not heard
This can't be destiny
Even the voice of the smallest bird
Seems to be louder than me

Oh, Lord let me make history
I want to be part of His-story

FAITH

Love abounds
Beauty unfolds
A feeling that's not lost within the night
Days beyond years
Together
There are yet many roads
More than blue highways
City byways
Travel on
Forever
Days beyond years
Let us travel on
Holding you
Holding me
No more tears
When time is through
We'll look back

LOVE OF A LIFETIME

Close enough to touch
But-A million miles away
Take you in my arms
And- Beg you to stay
Seen His love shine
Looking for a brighter day
Nothing is impossible; When Christ lights the way
Lost and empty
Your eyes show your pain
Oh, what I wouldn't do for you
To ease the internal rain
Seen His light shine
Looking for a brighter day
Nothing is impossible; When Christ lights the way
Love of a lifetime
Trapped behind a mask
My love of a lifetime
I'm here for you
You only need to ask
Seen His love shine
Looking for a brighter day
Nothing is impossible; When Christ lights the way
Seen His love shine
Looking for a brighter day
Nothing is impossible; When Christ lights the way
Nothing is impossible; When Christ lights the way
Seen His love shine
Looking for a brighter day
See
Nothing is impossible when Christ is on our side
Nothing is impossible when Christ lights our way

IT COULD BE

Love
Is eternal
Love
Knows no bounds
Oh, it feels like this could be
Heaven
Your beauty
Surrounds
Your love
Warmth, light, and glory
Immeasurable
Your mercy and grace
Abound
Oh, it feels like this could be heaven
Why is it my feet are still on the ground

ULTIMATE

Wrapped in the mystery of your love
Longing to see You
Open your arms
Wanting your touch
Nestle this frail Dove

Silently Needing
Holding back the tears
Silently screaming
I love you this much

In your arms sustain me
Lost in this love
Thoughts of you remain with me
Deepening Love
Tonight I pray; tonight I pray
To know love when it is before me
To feel your touch again
To feel your touch
I feel your touch again
Silently needing
Rolling back the years
Endlessly pleading
I need your love
I feel your touch

A love without demand
Breaking through the barriers
Like a castle of sand
The past washes away with the tide
When i'm in your arms
Messiah

THE GREATEST OF ALL

Fragile hearts ache
How long must they remain apart
Looking forward to a brand new start
The love of two
One shared by so few
Joined in friendship
Faith-Hope-Endless Love
They look to the One
The One from above
The two become one
A union that can never be undone
United through the Son
Sweet Love
More tender than dew drops and doves
His is the Greatest of all Loves

YOUR SONG

(Is there a reason I'm the happiest girl in town?)
I'm gonna lay it all down
Gonna lay it all down
I'm gonna lay it down
For You-
I'm gonna lay it down
Gonna lay it all down
I'm gonna lay it all down
It's true-
I wanna run
(No way I'm gonna hide)
Watch me run
Screaming all night long
"Everyone in town...
Lay it all down!!!"
Relinquish control before the devil takes his toll
Hand it over to the Man
The Man who can
(He Loves You)
(See the footprints in the sand)
He can turn it all around
Just leave it in his hands
Does it seem like all is lost
Jesus
He will be there to save you
He will never forsake you
Just gotta lay it all down
Gotta lay it all down
He loves you.
Jesus
(He's the reason I'm the happiest girl in town. I learned to lay it all down.)

LOVE WITHOUT END

Hold me near
Hold me dear
I'll show you a love stronger than death
Purifier's fire
Burning so strong
No evil can stand this flame
A love no man can tame
Built on the Rock of life
Be Still
Don't fear
Feel destiny near

DESTINY BOUND

Love-Laughter
Love of a lifetime
Thank You Jesus
True Love is mine
Forever knowing
With You I'm destiny bound
Here I can lay all my burdens down
There's no place I'd rather be going
On the road of salvation destiny bound
On my knees again
Calling your name, Jesus
What once was lost has been found
There is no sweeter sound
On the road of salvation destiny bound
No worries-No woes
That's what I'm looking forward to
As I'm overcoming all foes
On the road of salvation destiny bound
Earnestly seeking Your face
Eyes to the sky
Waiting on that cloud
No need to worry-No need to hurry
There's no race

It's just You and me
We'll meet face to face
On the road of salvation destiny bound
Bearing your name
I've never been so free-so sure
Singing it loud-Singing it proud
On the road to salvation destiny bound
Loving You-loving me
Loving You:
The Most High-God of Heaven-God of All
Lord of Lords-King of Kings
The Truth- The Only Way
On my knees calling your name
Jesus,
The One and Only
To You I pray
On the road of salvation destiny bound
I've found the Truth
I believe
"On the road of salvation destiny bound"
There's only one Truth, you'll find it

FOREVERMORE

True Love-True Love
Is there anything on Earth
Better-Closer
To being above
Things have a funny way of being
Through human eyes it's sometimes hard seeing
Once you battle time
You see it's not your friend
It leaves you sublime
When you feel it moving closer
Closing in
Knowing it's your end
You see things new
In very different shades and hues
Things pass by
You realize
What it is you could truly use
Love-Friendship-Kindness of heart
Far more precious than any…
Riches-Wealth-Expensive art
Reaching back through…
Fortune-Fame
Time-Space
Was there anything that lasted
When all was lost; One love was left
He remained
Truer than life itself
I found the meaning of it; Equal to nothing else
True Love-True Love
Nothing on Earth better
Nothing closer to above
One Man and His Endless Love

MORE THAN A DREAM

Thunder shakes the foundation; Rattling the core
You say, it's love
I say, he needs more
Never has he felt it- a love so strong
He can't understand
How could all have happened so wrong
Now he has nothing left to do
Listen to his sad song
Oh, as the days move closer
He prays
He prays she won't be gone
Oh, the time is not long
"Please Lord help me to hang on…
You see, I need her so
Why couldn't she let me know
I Love her so
I'm afraid she'll never know
I need her- I need her
Please Lord, let me see her…"
The rain falls down
Drenching the ground
Another tear
He wipes fog from the mirror
Another year
The tears race; Marking his face
Crying in the night
He longs to hold her tight
Thunder shakes the foundation; Rattling the core
The rain falls down
He is slowly opening the door

BELOVED
(Song of Songs)

I am His
And he is mine
Forever and a day and a day
My beloved is on His way
When he arrives
I'll be his
He will be mine
Everyday
Everyday

LOVE- FROM ABOVE

Love it has a surprise
Your heart already knows
Your love shows
You can see it in your eyes
Love-Love without lies
Watching it materialize
When it's real it opens as a rose
It's not hard to realize
The love of a lifetime
Within your grasp
Standing before you
No questions asked
Light my night; Enlighten my days
Lift my soul
Things only You know
It's natural to pray and praise
On our knees
For the one we love
Brought together again
We will not pretend
For we are one in Him
In love
As He loves
There is no sin
We're ready
Ready to begin
Begin life anew
Together with You
His arms wrapped around us
Cementing like glue
Forever He has joined us
Me to you!

Beautiful To You

Because you love me-
You love me, you do-
Because you love me,
Your Love is so true
I'm beautiful to You
Help me remember
When this world drags me down
I'm beautiful to You
Pulling myself up
It knocks me down
Again & Again
But...I won't give up
Because
I'm beautiful to you
Beautiful to You

SHATTERED

Tonight
Is it too late to begin
Tonight
You saved my life
Tonight
I was lost and forgotten
Hurt-Unloved
Then I remembered
Remembered your face
Forcing reality to set in
I heard your voice calling
Calling out my name
Carried by the wind
Love
Wrapping around me
Forgiving
Forgetting
My burden
My sin
Like a child in your arms
Protected by angels' wings
You take my breath away
Of your beauty Heaven sings
Is it too late to begin
In that desperate moment
As all hung in the balance
Shattering all ties that bind

I had to choose
What road to take
No way to win
I could only lose.
A life so unkind
It was then you appeared
Across the screen in my mind
How can it be
I can feel you here
I couldn't see what your love meant to me
Is it too late to begin
Like a child in your arms
Protected by angels' wings
You take my breath away
Of your beauty Heaven sings
Is it too late to begin
Thank you angel of grace
As long as I am
I will never forget your face
I couldn't see what your love meant to me
Is it too late to begin
Is it too late to begin

YOUR EYES

Fingers gliding through my hair
Your hands softly caressing my face
Directing my stare
My gaze drawn in by love
Pulling me in deep
Lost in your eyes
Lost in your touch
When our eyes meet
I see beauty
I feel complete
I look into your eyes
I see the greens of Erie
Flecks of burning embers
Randomly submitting
Each of their own accord
Entwined in a passionate dance
Hidden behind an earthly disguise
I can see Heaven in your eyes

EVERY SINGLE DAY

I never thought love could hurt this way
Passion-pain
An inextinguishable flame
This isn't a game
We're playing for keeps
Feels like we are running-Running out of time
Every single day I wonder…
Was there something I failed to say
Why can't the world see
Oh, what your love means to me
Missing you every single day
I'm so in love with You
That's where I find my rhyme
This isn't a game
We're playing for keeps
Feels like we are running-Running out of time
Missing you every single day
Every single day

A VERY SPECIAL YOU

Walking in the garden
My mind full of thought and prayer
My senses overflowing
I didn't notice you there
I was praying:
Something about Love-Something about Life-
Something about Hereafter-
Mostly, my heart rejoicing
And giving thanks to my Lord- my Master
Magically you appear; From out of the blue
Among the grasses
The sun's golden rays shimmering on your skin
Through your hair it dances
I find myself marveling at this sight that is you
Silently, I stood watching
Maybe you're lost in a dream
You didn't even know that I was there-
Clad in Ireland's green
Standing up near Old Glory
"Halleluiah"
I heard the angels sing
An answer to a prayer
Through rose colored glasses
You saw me watching
But, you'll never know just how much it meant-
To see you there
You left my heart soaring on eagle's wings-
Thank you for that moment; It was time well spent
Let me tell you,
You make me want to be a better woman
The Lord knows that day
You were Heaven sent-

GENUINE LOVE
(WHAT DO YOU NEED?)

I need a best friend
Don't need no lies
Don't need no using
I need you Baby
Throw away the pride
Humble yourself
Get down on those knees
I need somebody
Who will stay with me
Pray with me
Please
Pray with me Baby
Don't you know
You can still save the day
Be my hero Baby
Be here-Now
Pray
Get on those knees and pray

VICTORY AND GLORY

People praying
Praying in the midst of disaster
Amongst the devastation
Showing faith
Praising His name
Giving Him the glory
Letting Him write your story
The victory is the Lord's
The victory is the Lord's
Let us reap the sweet reward
For the greatest victory is the Lord's
Strong and Mighty
We know His name
Burning stronger
Burning like a fire out of control
There is nothing finer
Then the Lord
Let Him make you whole
Burning like a fire
Stronger than earthly desire
He's no fool
Tried and true
He will never leave you
Feeling blue
Give Him your troubles
He will give you His love
His love so true

I LOVE YOU GOD
BY
JEFFREY J.

I love you God
Diamonds in the sky
With God shinning in our eyes
Make his back better-Please God
Thank You God
Thank You for all this food You made
Thank You for making medicine for us
Rainbows shinning in God's eyes
Shinning in Jupiter
And Shinning in our eyes
Thank You for making santa so we can get presents
Rainbows shinning in santa's eyes
Thank You for making the Easter Bunny and St. Nick
Thank You for making dogs
Rainbows shine in dogs' eyes
Rainbows shine in God's eyes
Mommy Loves You
We Love You God
Everything shines at Jupiter and God and God's Mom
Jesus' mom lives with him
Help the cops get all the bad guys
Diamonds and rainbows sparkle in the cops eyes
And in our eyes and in God's eyes and his Mom's eyes
Mom loves You!

THE DANCE

The internal song of love
Still Remains
Stronger now
Love fans the flames
The external passes away
Love never ends
Love never fails
Love shines brighter than fantasy
Love prevails
Never ask yourself
Love
Love, does He have enough for me
You have the answer
The Truth
The nails
It's easy to see
Love shines brighter than fantasy

FADED GLORY

Stars fade
The world dismisses their days
No rhyme
No reason
Christ's Fire is still a blaze
An inextinguishable flame
Passion and pain within the heart and soul
Of a man without fame
Thoughts unspoken
I can feel you pray
Wash away the shame
Wash away the blame
Protect the hope
Protect the heart
Wash it away
Shed the external
Watch it pass away
The eternal song of love still remains
Stronger now
Love fans the flame

Never Wear Flip Flops in the Rain

ABOUT THE AUTHOR

Roisin Rzeznik

Roisin Rzeznik is best known by her pseudonym Roisin (Van gogh-Rzeznik). She is a Midwest, Milwaukee, Chicago area artist, writer, photographer, pragmatic philosopher, activist, and humanitarian. She has four children whom are now grown and a grandson.

 She enjoys creating....

Roisin is a versatile artist working with many mediums and experimental techniques...most prevalent are her paintings and an occasional block print or rare drawing. Her focus is on contemporary art, abstract expressionism, research, visual rhyme, and poetry.

A tremendous lover of the archaic, prose, and art world-wide. The artist was inspired at an early age by her mentors and their willingness to indulge, experiment, and instruct in a broad, diverse, and eclectic range of art, technique, and philosophy.

Over the years Roisin has spent her time highlighting Fair Trade, fighting for human rights, women's rights, children's rights, racial congruity, the abolition of extreme poverty, Aids, Malaria, human trafficking, and Genocide.

Roisin is known for often crediting her greatest loves as influences including God Himself; music as her muse and those whom create it.

Roisin credits Greg Dulli as the magical masterful genius whom constantly drives her to explore her artistic direction and often fill page upon page with verse. Of which, Filthy Sleaze (Out Damn Spot), her latest poem, which is said to illuminate the darkness surrounding human trafficking and other global and societal ills has been compared to Allen Ginsberg's Howl.

Roisin harbors a deep belief that, "Global Peace and Unity are achievable; They are a tangible gift from the Almighty."